To:
_____
_____

From:
_____
_____

Date:
_____

Little Miss Grace Prayer Book

© 2009 Christian Art Gifts, RSA
Christian Art Gifts Inc., IL, USA

Designed by Christian Art Gifts

Scripture verses are taken from the *Holy Bible*, Contemporary
English Version. Copyright © American Bible Society 1995.
Published in South Africa by the Bible Society of South Africa with
the permission of the American Bible Society.

Scripture verses are taken from the *Holy Bible*, New Living
Translation, copyright © 1996, 2004. Used by permission of
Tyndale House Publishers, Inc., Carol Stream, Illinois 60188.
All rights reserved.

Scripture verses are taken from *The Message*. Copyright © by
Eugene H. Peterson, 1993, 1994, 1995, 1996, 2000, 2001, 2002.
Used by permission of NavPress Publishing Group.

Scripture verses are taken from the *Holy Bible*, The New Century
Version®. Copyright © 1987, 1988, 1991. Used by permission of
Word Publishing. All rights reserved.

Printed in China

ISBN 978-1-77036-246-8

10 11 12 13 14 15 16 17 18 19 – 13 12 11 10 9 8 7 6 5 4

Little Miss
Grace

Prayer
Book

christian
art gifts®

Contents

Little Miss Grace ...

Little Miss Grace
Prays for Her Family

A family is one of God's masterpieces.

Anonymous

Parents Who Encourage

Dear God, thank You so much
for my parents. They believe
in me, and encourage me
to be the best that I can be.
That means a lot to me – even
if I don't always act like it does.

Amen.

Knowledge puffs you up
with pride, but love builds up.

1 Corinthians 8:1

My Precious Family

Dear God, please be with Mom
and Dad at work today.
Help me to do the best I can at school.
Be with my little brother and sister,
and all my other friends and family.
In Jesus' name.

Amen.

Whatever work you do, do your best.

Ecclesiastes 9:10

Obey Your Mom No Matter What

God, You know that sometimes it's
really hard for me to get along
with Mom. It feels like she just
doesn't get me. Help me to obey and
listen to Mom even if I think her
rules are way too strict.

Amen.

Honor your father and your mother as
the LORD your God has commanded you.
Then you will live a long time,
and things will go well for you.

Deuteronomy 5:16

Cut 'em Some Slack

Dear God, my dad works very hard. Sometimes he has to work till late at night, and we hardly get to see him. Help me to be good when he is around so that I can help to make his, and Mom's, life easier.

Amen.

Be kind and loving to each other, and forgive each other just as God forgave you in Christ.

Ephesians 4:32

A Happy Home

Dear God, many of my
friends come from really
unhappy homes.
Thank You for my happy home.
And thank You that
my mom and dad love
each other, and that
they love You most of all.

Amen.

My family and I are going to
worship and obey the LORD!

Joshua 24:15

Kindness Counts

Dear God, some days it's tough for me to be nice to my stepdad. He's really good to my mom, and to my brother and me. But I miss my real dad so much. Help me to be kind to him even when I don't feel like it.

Amen.

May the Lord make your love grow more and multiply for each other and for all people.

1 Thessalonians 3:12

Little Miss Grace
Talks to God About Her Friends

A true friend is someone who is there
for you when she'd rather be anywhere else.

Len Wein

Friends = Fun Times

Dear God, thank You for my friends. Having friends makes life more fun! Help me to always treat them right, and to be there for them when they need me. **Amen.**

Love each other like brothers and sisters.

Romans 12:10

Stand by Your Friends

Dear Father, my friend is moving
to another city. I'm going to miss her
so much. She is also sad to leave.
Help her to make friends in her new
school. Don't let her forget about me.

Amen.

Friends love through
all kinds of weather.

Proverbs 17:17

Laughter is the Best Medicine

Dear God, I had fun today!
My friends and I got the
giggles. Once we started to
laugh we couldn't stop.
It was hilarious. A good laugh
makes me feel good!
Thank You for inventing laughter.

Amen.

On your feet now – applaud GOD!
Bring a gift of laughter,
sing yourselves into His presence.

Psalm 100:1

Precious in God's Sight

Dear God, I've never thought about how other girls might feel if they're not accepted into my circle of friends. Help me to be loving, and to see other girls as You see them. You love us just the way we are, because we are all precious to You.

Amen.

People look at the outside of a person, but the LORD looks at the heart.

1 Samuel 16:7

Words can Hurt

Dear God, I had a big fight with
my best friend today.
I said some ugly things
that I didn't mean because
I was angry. Please forgive me.
Please help my friend to
forgive me too. She's my BFF.

Amen.

You use steel to sharpen steel,
and one friend sharpens another.

Proverbs 27:17

Keeping Score

Dear God, I was really hurt by what
my friend did to me. She said
nasty things about me behind my
back. Now I want to keep score!
Lord, please remind me that
life is not about getting even.
Help me to always see the bigger picture
when people are nasty for no reason.

Amen.

Live in peace with each other.
Do not be proud, but make friends
with those who seem unimportant.
Do not think how smart you are.

Romans 12:16

Little Miss Grace
Goes to God When Life Stinks

There are three stages in the work of God:
Impossible; Difficult; Done.

Hudson Taylor

Believe
in Yourself

Dear God, today was a hard day!
I doubted myself ... Please help me
to be more confident, and realize
that I am somebody because You
made me. And You never make junk!
In Jesus' name.

Amen.

Depend on the LORD; trust Him,
and He will take care of you.

Psalm 37:5

You Are Never Alone

Lord, sometimes I feel kinda lonely. Dad is working, Mom is busy – everyone has stuff to do. It feels as if there's no one to really hear me. But I know You do. You are always there for me. Thank You, Lord.

Amen.

God has said, "I will never leave you; I will never abandon you."

Hebrews 13:5

Pray About Everything

Dear God, I might not have
the perfect body, or the coolest
clothes, but I have You and
I know You love me! Help me to
see myself as You see me, perfectly
and wonderfully made!

Amen.

God has given each of
us different gifts to use.

Romans 12:6

Stressed Out

Dear God, I'm totally stressed out!
And the pressure to perform
sometimes gets me down.
I have to get good grades, do well
in sports, participate in the school
play … Help me to bring everything
that stresses me out to You.
I know You'll help me to cope.

Amen.

"If you are tired from carrying
heavy burdens, come to Me
and I will give you rest."

Matthew 11:28

When It's Hard to Cope

Dear Lord, my dad has been drinking
again … and then he shouts and
gets mad at everybody, especially at Mom.
Please help Dad to stop drinking.
Help us to make life easier for him.
In Jesus' name.

Amen.

"If you ask Me for anything
in My name, I will do it."

John 14:14

Forever and Always

God, life is sometimes so hard that it feels like You have turned Your back on me. Dad left Mom and me, money is tight and to top it all, my dog died. Please help me to remember that You always love me no matter what. You love me forever and always.

Amen.

What can we say about all this?
If God is on our side,
can anyone be against us?

Romans 8:31

Little Miss Grace
Obeys God and Others

You can never go wrong when
you choose to obey Christ.

Anonymous

Obey God Above All

Dear God, I know that I don't always
obey You like I should. I know it's wrong.
Please help me to make room in my
life for You, and not just for my best
friend and the stuff I like to do.
I want to be great at obeying You.

Amen.

Remind the people to obey the rulers
and authorities and not to be rebellious.
They must always be ready
to do something helpful.

Titus 3:1

Do You Match Up?

Dear God, sometimes I think I'm not doing too badly, but when I look at the Ten Commandments and how I obey them, I kind of stink! Please help me to keep Your rules and obey Your Word.

Amen.

"We will serve the LORD our God, and we will obey Him."

Joshua 24:24

Accept Your Family

Dear God, sometimes I get so mad at my parents. Some of their rules seem really ridiculous to me. To obey them is not always easy. Please help me.

Amen.

Watch what God does, and then you do it, like children who learn proper behavior from their parents.

Ephesians 5:1

Make a Stand

Dear God, I have to admit that I'm nervous sometimes about what my friends think of me being a Christian. Help me to get over it, and live boldly for You.

Amen.

You must choose for yourselves today whom you will serve.

Joshua 24:15

Worldly vs. Godly Things

Dear Lord, the messages that we get
from TV, magazines, and the Internet
are different from what You say in
Your Word. Help me to pay attention
to You and listen to Your voice instead
of listening to the world's messages.

Amen.

"I have told you all this so
that you may have peace in Me.
Here on earth you will have many
trials and sorrows. But take heart,
because I have overcome the world."

John 16:33

Patience

Dear God, patience doesn't always come easily to me. I guess I spend too much time thinking about myself and what I want. Help me to obey You by being patient with others and with situations that I can't change.

Amen.

Keep in step with God's love, as you wait for the Lord Jesus Christ to show how kind He is by giving you eternal life.

Jude 21

Little Miss Grace
Praises God for His Greatness

A person's chief work is the praise of God.

St. Augustine

Praise Him!

Dear God, I praise You for all the
wonderful things You created.
I praise You for butterflies, flowers,
mountains and the ocean.
Thank You for friends and family.
I praise You for loving me and caring for me.

Amen.

LORD our Lord, Your name is the most
wonderful name in all the earth!
It brings You praise in heaven above.

Psalm 8:1

Starry Skies

God, tonight I looked up at the dark sky and saw thousands of shining stars. What You've created is so awesome! Thank You that You are in control of the whole universe! You are so great. In Jesus' name. Amen.

God looked at everything He had made, and it was very good.

Genesis 1:31

God Just Loves Your Praises

Dear Lord, I feel great today!
Nothing big is happening.
I just feel Your presence
and it's amazing!
Thanks for taking care of me!
In Jesus' name.

Amen.

It is good to sing praises to our God;
it is good and pleasant to praise Him.

Psalm 147:1

Make a Difference

Dear God, I praise You for helping me and being with me all the time! Help me to look to You when I have to make difficult choices. I want to give You the time and energy You need from me to make a difference in people's lives.

Amen.

You are wonderful, LORD, and You deserve all praise, because You are much greater than anyone can understand.

Psalm 145:3

In Control

Thank You, God, for the little
reminders in life that show me
that You're still in control.
Help me to see the many, many
wonderful things in Your creation.
I praise You as the King of my
life and of the whole earth.

Amen.

Our LORD and Ruler, Your name
is wonderful everywhere on earth!
You let Your glory be seen
in the heavens above.

Psalm 8:1

Let the Good Times Roll

Dear Lord, thank You for a great day today with friends, food and fun. I know that not every day will be as perfect as this one, but I know that You are perfect, and that You make good times possible! Help me not to take the good things in my life for granted. In Jesus' name.

Amen.

Anyone who is having troubles should pray. Anyone who is happy should sing praises.

James 5:13

45

Little Miss Grace
Says, "Thank You"

This day and your life are God's gift to you:

so give thanks and be joyful always!

Jim Beggs

Thank You, God!

Dear God, thank You for looking at my heart, and not at the stupid things I say and do sometimes! I want You to be pleased with my life. Thank You for giving me chance after chance!

Amen.

Give thanks to the God of heaven. His love continues forever.

Psalm 136:26

Awesome Love

Dear Father, I'm so thankful that
I can come to You with my
prayers any time, and that I know
You are always there for me.
Thank You for Your awesome love.

Amen.

The LORD is merciful! He is kind
and patient, and His love never fails.

Psalm 103:8

God Cares About Every Little Detail

Dear God, You know me inside out.
You know when I'm sad or happy.
You know when I've done something
great or something not so good.
Thank You for knowing me so well,
and still loving me.

Amen.

LORD, I trust You. I have said, "You
are my God." My life is in Your hands.

Psalm 31:14-15

Remember to Be Thankful

Dear God, please forgive me when I forget to thank You. I have so much to be thankful for in life. Forgive my selfishness, and help me to be thankful to You and to others. In Jesus' name.

Amen.

Thank the LORD and praise His name.

Psalm 100:4

God's Wonderful Creation

Dear God, today I just want to thank You
for all the totally amazing things
You've created. Thank You for peace
and happiness, and that I'm healthy and
happy. Thank You for newborn babies,
plants and animals. Most of all, God,
I want to thank You for Your love.

Amen.

The heavens declare the glory of God, and
the skies announce what His hands have made.

Psalm 19:1

Care 4 Creation

Thank You, Lord, for the beauty, wonder
and mystery of creation. We often take
so much of Your works for granted.
Help me as Your child to look after
Your creation, and to take time to appreciate
all the wonderful things around me.

Amen.

The Lord is good to everyone.
He showers compassion on all His creation.

Psalm 145:9

Little Miss Grace
Says, "I'm Sorry, God"

Forgiveness is the key to happiness.

Anonymous

Take Responsibility

Dear God, okay, I admit it. I've made some really dumb choices and they are the reasons for some of the problems in my life. Help me to clean up my act, and to make better choices.

Amen.

Remember the LORD in all you do, and He will give you success.

Proverbs 3:6

Keep Your Cool

Lord, I'm so sorry. I lost my temper …
again. It's so hard not to get mad at my
brother when he teases me all the time.
Help me to be nice to him even when
he's horrible to me.

Amen.

God gave us this command:
Those who love God must also love their
brothers and sisters.

1 John 4:21

Saying You're Sorry

Lord Jesus, please forgive me.
Today I felt jealous and grumpy.
I said things that were spiteful and
unkind to some kids at school.
Help me to apologize to them
and to make things better.

Amen.

People with quick tempers cause
trouble, but those who control their
tempers stop a quarrel.

Proverbs 15:18

When Others Hurt You

Dear God, it is very hard to forgive people who have hurt my friends or me. Sometimes I want to hurt them back. But You taught us to love others even when they hurt us. Help me to understand why people say and do hurtful things. And help me to love them.

Amen.

You are a forgiving God. You are kind and full of mercy. You do not become angry quickly, and You have great love.

Nehemiah 9:17

Today Is Your Best Day

God, I've done many wrong things today again. Please forgive my sins because of Jesus who died on the cross in my place. Thank You for Jesus, for daily forgiveness, and for each new day to make a fresh start.

Amen.

This is the day the LORD has made;
let us rejoice and be glad in it.

Psalm 118:24

Forgiveness Sets Me Free

Heavenly Father, thank You for showing me the importance of forgiveness in all the relationships of my life. And thank You for Your promise to forgive me. I am happy because You have forgiven me, and I want to forgive others as well. In Jesus' name.

Amen.

> Forgive anyone who does you wrong, just as Christ has forgiven you.
>
> Colossians 3:13

Little Miss Grace
Knows That God's Love Is Real Love

Love puts the fun in together,

the sad in apart,

and the joy in the heart.

Anonymous

True Love

Dear God, I'm happy that You love me.
I pray that I may never forget
how much it pleases You when
I am happy, and good, and do positive things
that make a difference in other people's lives.

Amen.

God is love. This is how God showed His love
among us: He sent His one and only Son
into the world that we might live through Him.

1 John 4:8-9

Love Like Jesus

I love You, Jesus. How can I thank You
enough for dying on the cross for me?
Help me to love others the way You love them,
and to follow in Your perfect steps of love.

Amen.

> "Love each other. You must love
> each other as I have loved you."
>
> John 13:34

Imitate God ...

Dear God, help me to make good choices
that show Your love in my life. Help me
to live in such a way that others can see
my love for You in the things I say and do.

Amen.

You are God's children whom He loves,
so try to be like Him. Live a life of love
just as Christ loved us and gave
Himself for us as a sweet-smelling
offering and sacrifice to God.

Ephesians 5:1-2

Matters of the Heart

Lord, there is some stuff in my heart that is not good. Help me to clean my heart of bad things, and fill me with love for You and others. In Jesus' name.

Amen.

"Good people do good things because of the good in their hearts.
Bad people do bad things because of the evil in their hearts.
Your words show what is in your heart."

Luke 6:45

God's Gift

Dear God, I choose to accept Jesus into my heart today. Please forgive my sins, and help me to obey You. Thank You for Your gift of love to us – Your Son, Jesus.

Amen.

"Anyone who believes
in God's Son has eternal life."

John 3:36

Top Priority

Dear God, help me to get my priorities straight. I want to love You above everything else in my life. I want to love You with my whole heart, soul and mind. I don't want other stuff to take Your place in my life. You are my #1 priority.

Amen.

Jesus answered, "Love the Lord your God with all your heart, all your soul, and all your mind. This is the first and most important command."

Matthew 22:37-38

Little Miss Grace
Speaks to God
About Growing Up

If the shoe fits, you're not allowing for growth.

Robert N. Coons

Grow Up!

Dear God, growing up is hard. I have to do things that I don't feel like. And sometimes I feel like throwing a temper tantrum when I don't get what I want. But I know that You want me to control my actions and my words. Help me to grow up.

Amen.

Don't be like the people of this world,
but let God change the way you think.
Then you will know how to do everything
that is good and pleasing to Him.

Romans 12:2

Your Future Is Bright

Dear God, You know what's best for me.
Help me not to worry about
what's going to happen tomorrow.
Because You love us so much,
I know You'll take care of everything.

Amen.

"Don't worry about tomorrow,
for tomorrow will bring its own worries.
Today's trouble is enough for today."

Matthew 6:34

Stay
Pure

Dear God, I hear about sex all the time from TV, music, movies, and even from some of my friends. Help me to stay strong, and to keep myself pure. Help me to remember that You created sex as something special between a husband and wife.

Amen.

Keep yourself pure.

1 Timothy 5:22

Are You a Worrywart?

Lord, I sometimes worry about a lot of things. I worry about the future. I worry about whether I will get good grades in school, and if I'll be accepted into college one day. I worry about making the school choir and the tennis team. Help me not to worry about anything, but to pray about everything.

Amen.

Don't worry about anything, but pray about everything. With thankful hearts offer up your prayers and requests to God.

Philippians 4:6

The Unknown

Dear God, new things and situations scare me. Like when I had to go to a new school and when we went to a new church. Thank You that You are always with me, and that You are always the same. Help me to be brave and face new challenges knowing that You are by my side.

Amen.

GOD said, "My presence will go with you. I'll see the journey to the end."

Exodus 33:14

Guys and Girls Are Just ... Different

God, guys and girls are so totally different from each other. Guys like fast cars and sports, and we like to giggle and dress up. But thank You, God, for the wonderful differences between us that still make us like each other.

Amen.

You made my whole being;
You formed me in my mother's body.
I praise You because You made me
in an amazing and wonderful way.
What You have done is wonderful.

Psalm 139:13-14

Little Miss Grace
Asks God's Help to Resist Temptations

When you flee temptation,
don't leave a forwarding address.

Anonymous

Jesus Knows

Jesus, thank You that You really understand what we have to go through on earth. Temptations are everywhere, every day. To be able to resist all the temptations of the world, one must be really strong. Jesus, please help me fight off temptations, like You did.

Amen.

You can trust God, who will not permit you
to be tempted more than you can stand.
But when you are tempted, He will also give you a
way to escape so that you will be able to stand it.

1 Corinthians 10:13

Make Wise Choices

Dear God, some choices in life aren't easy,
and it's difficult to know right from wrong.
Help me to always come to You when
I have to make difficult choices in life.
And even with the small stuff.

Amen.

If you need wisdom, ask our generous God,
and He will give it to you.

James 1:5

Sneaking Around

Dear God, to know that the devil is sneaking around to find someone to attack is kind of scary! Please help me to be on my guard and to resist the devil when he tempts me.

Amen.

Be on your guard and stay awake.
Your enemy, the devil, is like a roaring lion,
sneaking around to find someone to attack.

1 Peter 5:8

A Role to Play

God, whether I'm the strong, quiet type
or the talkative kind, I know that I have
a role to play in Your kingdom. Help me
to talk about You and tell others about
Your wonderful love for us. Thank You for
noticing when I do something well, and
smiling when I do something silly.

Amen.

Teach us to use wisely
all the time we have.

Psalm 90:12

The World Wide Web

Dear God, as children in today's information age all knowledge and information is literally at our fingertips. Help me to remember that knowledge does not always lead to wisdom. Please protect me from negative information and temptations when I surf the Web.

Amen.

Do all you can to live a peaceful life. Take care of your own business, and do your own work. If you do, then people who are not believers will respect you.

1 Thessalonians 4:11-12

Against the Tide

Dear God, to go against the tide is not easy. Thank You for people throughout history who have sacrificed everything to stand up for their faith.
Please help me to take a stand against things that do not please You.

Amen.

Be alert. Continue strong in the faith.
Have courage, and be strong.

1 Corinthians 16:13

Little Miss Grace
Follows in Jesus' Steps

If you haven't learned to follow,

you can't lead.

Henriettea C. Mears

In His Footsteps

Dear God, thank You for Your awesome love.
I see it all around me, and I feel it in my heart.
I want to love others like You love us.
Help me to live like Jesus did, so that I can
make the world around me a better place.

Amen.

Live a life filled with love, following the
example of Christ. He loved us and
offered Himself as a Sacrifice for us,
a pleasing aroma to God.

Ephesians 5:2

A Friend in Jesus

Jesus, please forgive me for the times
when I have turned friendship with
You down because friendship with the
world seemed more important and
looked more attractive. Thank You for
loving me so much that You sacrificed
Your life to fix my relationship with God.

Amen.

You should know that loving the world is the
same as hating God. Anyone who wants to be
a friend of the world becomes God's enemy.

James 4:4

89

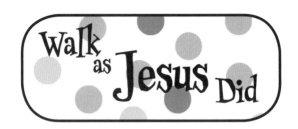

Walk as Jesus Did

Dear Lord, I don't want to lose my friends,
but I also don't want to do some of the wrong
things they do. Help me to love them, but to
still act as an ambassador of Jesus.
Help me to do what Jesus did – not to
withdraw myself from people who sin,
but to distance *myself* from sin.

Amen.

Whoever says that he lives
in God must live as Jesus lived.

1 John 2:6

The Best Example

Living Lord Jesus, thank You that You are the great Conqueror. But at the same time, You also modeled great humility. Teach me to live a victorious but humble life in You.

Amen.

Be humble under God's powerful hand so He will lift you up when the right time comes.

1 Peter 5:6

No Performance Required

Dear Lord Jesus, I'm so glad that I don't have to perform to be part of Your 'group'. You welcome me just the way I am. Thank You that I matter to You.

Amen.

"I no longer call you servants, because a servant does not know what his master is doing. But I call you friends, because I have made known to you everything I heard from My Father."

John 15:15

Don't Judge a Book by Its Cover

Dear Jesus, You show us time and again in the Bible that You loved outsiders with Your whole heart. Please help me not to judge others by their appearances. I want to follow Your example.

Amen.

Always be gentle with others.

Philippians 4:5

Little Miss Grace
Wants to Be
the Best That She Can Be

You have within you all the elements that
are necessary to make you all the Father
dreamed that you would be in Christ.

E. W. Kenyon

The Best Role Model Ever

Dear Jesus, thank You for loving me. You are the best! You never let me down. You forgive my sins, and You are always there when things are tough. I want to be more like You.

Amen.

When we have the opportunity to help anyone, we should do it.

Galatians 6:10

My Best for God

Dear God, You are loving and kind. Thank You for always keeping Your promises. Please help me to always do my best for You. In Jesus' name.

Amen.

LORD, God of Israel, there is no god like You in heaven above or on earth below. You keep Your agreement of love with Your servants who truly follow You.

1 Kings 8:23

Beautiful in God's Eyes

Dear God, I want to be skinny and beautiful.
But please give me the courage to accept
the things that I cannot change,
and to change what I can.
Above all, help me to see that good looks
are not the only thing that counts.
Make my heart beautiful.
Amen.

Don't depend on things like fancy hairdos or
gold jewelry or expensive clothes to make you
look beautiful. Be beautiful in your heart by being
gentle and quiet. This kind of beauty will last,
and God considers it very special.

1 Peter 3:3-4

What to Choose?

Dear Lord, to make good choices is difficult. Especially when the wrong option seems very appealing. Help me to weigh my options before I make decisions, and to make them in light of my Christian values.

Amen.

Listen carefully to what wise people say; pay attention to what I am teaching you.
It will be good to keep these things in mind so that you are ready to repeat them.

Proverbs 22:17-18

A Listening Ear

Dear God, please give me a heart for other people, and a listening ear to hear what they really want to tell me. Give me patience so that I won't be so quick to take offense when I don't agree with others.

Amen.

My dear friends, you should be quick to listen and slow to speak or to get angry.

James 1:19

Wake Up Call

Dear God, some kids at my school
think it is cool to use drugs.
But I don't want to fall in that trap.
I pray for every young girl who is
caught up in the web of drugs.
Make me strong to encourage
others never to use drugs.

Amen.

God will judge everything we do,
even what is done in secret,
whether good or bad.

Ecclesiastes 12:14

Little Miss Grace
Is the Apple of God's Eye

God loves each one of us
as if there were only one of us.

St. Augustine

God's Favorite

Dear God, Your grace and mercy are amazing. In my own eyes I feel worthless, but with You I am #1. Thank You that You love me not because I'm great at sports or math, but because I belong to You.

Amen.

The Spirit Himself joins with our spirits to say we are God's children.

Romans 8:16

Born Again

Dear Jesus, what a miracle and
an honor to have You live in
my heart. Make me worthy of You.

Amen.

A child has been born to us;
God has given a Son to us. He will be
responsible for leading the people.
His name will be Wonderful Counselor,
Powerful God, Father Who Lives Forever,
Prince of Peace.

Isaiah 9:6

Awesome Plans

Dear God, I'm so glad that You are in control of all things! I know that Your plans for me are all good. Thank You that I can trust You with my life.

Amen.

The LORD keeps you from all harm and watches over your life. The LORD keeps watch over you as you come and go, both now and forevermore.

Psalm 121:7-8

A Worry-Free Life

Dear God, it's so amazing that You care
about the things that worry me – even
the really small things. Thank You that
I can bring all my worries to You.

Amen.

God cares for you, so turn all
your worries over to Him.

1 Peter 5:7

In My Place

God, it must have hurt so much to see what Jesus had to go through on the cross for our sins. Thank You, Lord, for loving me so much that You gave Your Son to die in my place. Your grace and mercy are awesome.

Amen.

"I love you people with a love that will last forever. That is why I have continued showing you kindness."

Jeremiah 31:3

Big Love

Dear God, Your love for me is so great that I can't imagine it for myself. Help me to see more of Your love every day in the world around me. Thank You for loving me so much that You call me Your child.

Amen.

The Father has loved us so much that we are called children of God. And we really are His children.

1 John 3:1

Little Miss Grace Speaks to God About Girls' Issues

Let God's promises shine on your problems.

Corrie ten Boom

Time to Cool Down

Dear God, I need Your help and guidance in my relationship with my boyfriend. Give me the strength to stick to what I want for us. Give me the insight to avoid situations where things between us go too far.

Amen.

So I tell you: Live by following the Spirit. Then you will not do what your sinful selves want.

Galatians 5:16

Miss Popular

Dear God, I want to be popular
at school, but please help me not
to do it at Your expense.
Please give me insight and the right
attitude to act in the right way.
Help me to allow others their
chance to feel popular too.

Amen.

Don't be conceited or make
others jealous by claiming
to be better than they are.

Galatians 5:26

Little Lies ...

Lord, I know it's wrong to lie, but when it comes to telling lies to my parents and teachers to save me from trouble, I don't think about it. I just do it. Please help me not to lie, even if it's just a little white lie to my friend.

Amen.

"Whoever can be trusted with a little can also be trusted with a lot, and whoever is dishonest with a little is dishonest with a lot."

Luke 16:10

Loneliness

Dear God, I feel lonely and I hate it!
It feels like no one notices or even
knows me. But You know me, Lord.
Teach me not to wait on others to
do things for me, but to reach out
to them. Thank You that I can always
count on You. In Jesus' name.

Amen.

"Don't worry, because I am with you.
Don't be afraid, because I am your God.
I will make you strong and will help you; I will
support you with My right hand that saves you."

Isaiah 41:10

Weight Issues

Lord, weight is an issue for girls!
Help me not to become obsessed with
my weight. Remind me that You don't
measure us like the world does, and that
my confidence lies in the fact that You
know me and love me just the way I am.

Amen.

Use good sense and measure yourself by
the amount of faith that God has given you.

Romans 12:3

Guard My Tongue

Dear God, I feel ashamed of the bad language that comes out of my mouth sometimes when I try to show off in front of my friends. Please forgive me, and guard my tongue. I want to make You proud by my words.

Amen.

"Your words show what is in your hearts."

Matthew 12:34

Little Miss Grace
Prays from the Bible

In prayer it is better to have a heart
without words than words without a heart.

John Bunyan

The Lord's Prayer

"Our Father in heaven,
Hallowed be Your name.
Your kingdom come.
Your will be done
On earth as it is in heaven.
Give us this day our daily bread,
And forgive us our debts,
As we forgive our debtors.
And do not lead us into temptation,
But deliver us from the evil one.
For Yours is the kingdom
And the power and the glory,
forever."

Amen.

Matthew 6:9-13

Prayer for Bedtime

I can lie down
and sleep soundly
because You,
LORD, will keep me safe.

Psalm 4:8

God My Maker

I praise You because You made me
in an amazing and wonderful way.
What You have done is wonderful.
You saw my bones being formed
as I took shape in my mother's body.
When I was put together there,
You saw my body as it was formed.
All the days planned for me were written
in Your book before I was one day old.
God, Your thoughts are precious to me.
They are so many! If I could count them,
they would be more
than all the grains of sand.
When I wake up, I am still with You.

Psalm 139:14-18

Trust in God

Fig trees may no longer bloom,
or vineyards produce grapes;
olive trees may be fruitless,
and harvest time a failure;
sheep pens may be empty,
and cattle stalls vacant –
but I will still celebrate
because the LORD God saves me.

Habakkuk 3:17-18

The Prayer of Jabez

Please do good things for me and give me more land. Stay with me, and don't let anyone hurt me. Then I won't have any pain. And God did what Jabez had asked.

1 Chronicles 4:10

The Lord's Wonderful Love

With all my heart
I praise the LORD, and with all that I am
I praise His holy name!
With all my heart I praise the LORD!
I will never forget how kind He has been.
The LORD forgives our sins,
heals us when we are sick,
and protects us from death.
His kindness and love are a crown on our heads.
Each day that we live, He provides for our needs
and gives us the strength of a young eagle.

Psalm 103:1-5

God's Promises

Sometimes you have days where nothing goes right. **Turn to God!** He loves you and is waiting to help you. Read these verses whenever you need a little bit of love, forgiveness, joy or encouragement. **God is your Friend** and will be there for you always.

When I Need Help

- "Call to Me in times of trouble. I will save you." Psalm 50:15 NCV
- I pray to You, God, because You will help me. Listen and answer my prayer! Psalm 17:6 CEV
- I know the LORD is always with me. I will not be shaken, for He is right beside me. No wonder my heart is glad, and I rejoice. My body rests in safety. Psalm 16:8-9 NLT
- The LORD is good to those who depend on Him. Lamentations 3:25 NLT

When I Have No Clue What to Do

- "For I know the plans I have for you," declares the LORD, "plans to prosper you and not to harm you, plans to give you hope and a future." Jeremiah 29:11 NIV
- The LORD will work out His plans for my life. Psalm 138:8 NLT
- Show me the right path, O LORD; point out the road for me to follow. Psalm 25:4 NLT
- Trust GOD from the bottom of your heart; don't try to figure out everything on your own. Listen for GOD's voice in everything you do, everywhere you go; He's the one who will keep you on track. Proverbs 3:5-6 The Message

When I Need a Hug

- The LORD is there to rescue all who are discouraged and have given up hope. Psalm 34:18 CEV

- May our Lord Jesus Christ Himself and God our Father encourage you and strengthen you in every good thing you do and say. God loved us, and through His grace He gave us a good hope and encouragement that continues forever. 2 Thessalonians 2:16-17 NCV

- The Lord has promised that He will not leave us or desert us. Hebrews 13:5 CEV

- "I will comfort you as a mother comforts her child." Isaiah 66:13 NCV

When I Need a Friend

- "I will be with you, day after day after day, right up to the end of the age." Matthew 28:20 The Message

- Even when I walk through the darkest valley, I will not be afraid, for You are close beside me. Psalm 23:4 NLT

- God has said, "I will never leave you; I will never abandon you." Hebrews 13:5 NCV

- "I will be with you and bless you." Genesis 26:3 NLT

When I Need to Be Brave

Be strong and courageous. Do not be terrified; do not be discouraged, for the LORD your God will be with you wherever you go. Joshua 1:9 NIV

If God is for us, no one can defeat us. Romans 8:31 NCV

God will command His angels to protect you wherever you go. They will carry you in their arms, and you won't hurt your feet on the stones. Psalm 91:11-12 CEV

"Don't be afraid, for I am with you. Don't be discouraged, for I am your God. I will strengthen you and help you. I will hold you up with My victorious right hand." Isaiah 41:10 NLT

When I Need a Bit of Hope

- This is the day the Lord has made; let us rejoice and be glad in it. Psalm 118:24 NIV
- The Lord is my strength and my song. Psalm 118:14 NLT
- I am overwhelmed with joy in the Lord my God! Isaiah 61:10 NLT
- God will take delight in you with gladness. With His love, He will calm all your fears. He will rejoice over you with joyful songs. Zephaniah 3:17 NLT

When I Need to Forgive

- "Love your neighbor as yourself." Matthew 19:19 NIV
- Be kind and compassionate to one another, forgiving each other. Ephesians 4:32 NIV
- Make allowance for each other's faults, and forgive anyone who offends you. Remember, the Lord forgave you, so you must forgive others. Colossians 3:13 NLT
- "And when you stand praying, if you hold anything against anyone, forgive him, so that your Father in heaven may forgiv you your sins." Mark 11:25 NIV

When I Feel Guilty

- Do you think anyone is going to be able to drive a wedge between us and Christ's love for us? There is no way! Not trouble, not hard times, not hatred, not bullying threats, not backstabbing, not even the worst sins. Romans 8:38-39 The Message
- "Though your sins are like scarlet, I will make them as white a snow. Though they are red like crimson, I will make them as white as wool." Isaiah 1:18 NLT
- Lord, You willingly forgive, and Your love is always there for those who pray to You. Psalm 86:5 CEV
- So I confessed my sins and told them all to You. I said, "I'll tell the Lord each one of my sins." Then You forgave me and took away my guilt. Psalm 32:5 CEV